ANDREW HENRY

INSTANT POT INDIAN COOKBOOK

Authentic Indian Flavors Made Effortless with Your Instant Pot (2024)

First edition

This book was professionally typeset on Reedsy.
Find out more at reedsy.com

Contents

1

Introduction

India boasts one of the largest and most influential civilizations globally, and it is widely recognized that Indians have a strong passion for food. Their enthusiasm for discussing cooking, experimenting with various recipes, and savoring diverse flavors is well-known. Indian cuisine encompasses a rich blend of both modern and traditional dishes from the Indian subcontinent. This culinary diversity is a result of the country's vast landscapes, varied climates, historical influences, diverse ethnic groups, and professions, all contributing significantly to the differences in Indian cuisine.

Indian culinary traditions have evolved through extensive cultural exchanges with neighboring regions such as Persia, ancient Greece, Mongols, and West Asia. This blending of flavors has not only influenced regional cuisines but has also inspired culinary traditions worldwide, especially in South East Asia. Today, Indian cuisine has become incredibly popular globally, delighting not only Indians but also people from North America, Europe, Australia, and Africa.

What sets Indian cuisine apart is its slow-cooking techniques and bold flavors. Pot cooking plays a crucial role in bringing out a wide range of tastes from various ingredients and seasonings, harmoniously merging them into delectable dishes. However, the intricate flavors of Indian cuisine don't mean that cooking has to be time-consuming. With the help of modern kitchen appliances like the instant pot, one can easily prepare all their favorite Indian dishes without sacrificing much time and effort. Are you familiar with the concept of an instant pot?

The Instant Pot stands as a versatile, all-in-one pressure cooker capable of preparing a wide array of dishes, spanning from breakfast items and desserts to meats, all in significantly less time than traditional stoves. With a variety of Instant Pot models available, each comes with its unique set of features, making it an essential kitchen companion. There are several compelling reasons why the Instant Pot has gained immense popularity, making it a kitchen essential worth considering.

First and foremost, the Instant Pot is more than just an electric pressure cooker. Functioning as a genuine multi-cooker, it can sear, brown, stir-fry, and even steam delicate items like seafood, eggs, and vegetables. Unlike old-fashioned manual pressure cookers, the Instant Pot operates smoothly, ensuring safety through preset limits. Whether you're a vegan, vegetarian, egg enthusiast, chicken lover, or a fan of goat or pork meat, the Instant Pot caters to all culinary preferences. It has made the preparation of Indian cuisines remarkably convenient, enabling anyone to prepare these dishes in the comfort of their home.

In this guide, you will discover a multitude of delectable Instant Pot Indian recipes that cover breakfast, lunch, dinner, snacks, and vegetarian options, offering a delightful culinary experience.

2

Chapter 01: Instant Pot Indian Breakfast Recipes

Discover a delightful assortment of Instant Pot Indian Breakfast Recipes that not only save you time but are also incredibly convenient for everyone. Dive into these mouthwatering recipes that can be effortlessly prepared at home, making your mornings a culinary delight.

❖ Instant Pot Hash

Preparation Time: 10 minutes

Cooking Time: 30 minutes

Servings: 5

Ingredients:

- Three tablespoons of butter
- One cup of minced yellow onion
- One cup of diced green bell pepper
- One cup of diced red bell pepper
- Four teaspoons of diced garlic cloves

- ½ tablespoon of dry sage
- ½ tablespoon of dried thyme
- Salt and pepper to taste
- One sliced potato
- Two cups of chicken broth

Instructions:

1. Press the sauté button on the Instant Pot and set the timer for 5 minutes.
2. Heat the butter in the pot. Add minced vegetables and cook, stirring regularly, for about 5 minutes until softened. Add all the spices and continue stirring for 2 minutes.
3. Turn off the sauté function. Add broth and potatoes, then lock the lid securely.
4. Set the timer for 15 minutes and press the sauté button again.
5. Stir occasionally until it boils. After 5 minutes, turn off the Instant Pot. Your Hash is ready to serve. Enjoy it with your choice of sides.

❖ Instant Pot Dhokla Buckwheat Corn

Servings: 5

Cooking Time: 35 minutes

Ingredients:

- Two minced green chilies
- 1 chopped ginger
- ½ teaspoon of baking soda

- 2 teaspoons of fruit salt
- ½ teaspoon of turmeric powder
- 2 tablespoons of sunflower oil
- 1/3 cup of water
- 2 cups of gram (besan) flour
- 1 cup of water (or more as needed)
- 2 teaspoons of salt to taste

Instructions:

1. Prepare all the ingredients and grease a cake tray or Dhokla plate.
2. Whisk the ingredients together, adding lemon zest and baking soda to froth up the Dhokla batter. Pour the batter into the greased plate and place it in the Instant Pot.
3. Steam the Khaman Dhokla and let it cool completely. Soak the tempering in the Dhokla for thorough absorption.

Embrace these delightful recipes and transform your mornings with the enticing flavors of Indian cuisine, all prepared conveniently in your Instant Pot. Enjoy your breakfast culinary adventures!

❖ Instant Pot Steel Cut Oats

Cooking Time: 40 minutes

Servings: 5

Ingredients:

- Two cups of steel-cut oats
- Three cups of water
- Two cups of milk
- ½ tablespoon of cinnamon
- Salt to taste

For serving:

- Two tablespoons of maple syrup or honey
- One teaspoon of vanilla extract
- Two bananas, diced
- Blueberries, diced
- Diced almonds

Instructions:

1. In the Instant Pot, combine oats, water, milk, cinnamon, and salt.
2. Set the Instant Pot to high pressure for 5 minutes. Sauté briefly.
3. Stir in the vanilla extract and turn off the Instant Pot.
4. Serve the oats with maple syrup, strawberries, blueberries, and almonds.

❖ Instant Pot Vegetable Rava Upma

Cooking Time: 20 minutes

Servings: 2

Ingredients:

- One cup of semolina (rava)
- One sliced onion
- ¼ cup of peas
- One cup of mixed vegetables
- Three green chilies, sliced
- One tablespoon of ginger, sliced
- ½ teaspoon of urad dal
- ¼ teaspoon of mustard seeds
- Fresh coriander leaves
- One tablespoon of oil
- Salt to taste

Instructions:

1. Heat the Instant Pot.
2. Prepare the vegetables on a cutting board.
3. In the Instant Pot, add the chopped vegetables and other ingredients. Mix well.
4. Add enough water and salt. Close the lid, seal the pressure valve, and pressure cook for 5-7 minutes.
5. After cooking, stir and transfer to a serving bowl.
6. Garnish with cashews.

❖ Instant Pot Upma Semolina with Coconut

Cooking Time: 30 minutes

Servings: 4

Ingredients:

- One cup of semolina
- Two teaspoons of ghee
- One teaspoon of mustard seeds
- Asafetida to taste
- One tablespoon of Chana dal and Urad dal (soaked for 10 minutes)
- One tablespoon of diced ginger
- One small red onion, sliced
- One green chili, diced
- Seven curry leaves
- Four tablespoons of green peas
- Two cups of water
- Salt to taste
- Two teaspoons of minced cilantro
- One teaspoon of oil

Instructions:

1. Roast semolina in the Instant Pot using sauté mode for 5 minutes.
2. Add two tablespoons of oil and all the ingredients. Stir for 5 minutes.
3. For a touch of sweetness, add honey or sugar.
4. Close the lid, seal the pressure valve, and pressure cook for 5-7 minutes.
5. Add ghee, turn off the Instant Pot, and mix well.
6. Serve with coconut chutney.

❖ Instant Puffed Upma Rice

Servings: 2

Cooking Time: 15 minutes

Ingredients:

- Three cups of puffed rice
- One small onion, chopped
- One small tomato, diced
- 1-2 green chilies
- ½ teaspoon of turmeric powder

- ½ teaspoon of mustard seeds
- A couple of curry leaves
- Two tablespoons of oil
- Salt to taste

Instructions:

1. Rinse the puffed rice thoroughly with running water, squeezing out excess water, and return it to the plate.
2. Switch on the sauté mode. Heat oil, add mustard seeds, and fry for 2 minutes.
3. Add spices, vegetables, and other ingredients.
4. Seal the Instant Pot, set the pressure valve to sealing, and pressure cook for 5-7 minutes.
5. Stir well upon opening the lid.
6. Serve the puffed upma rice immediately.

❖ Instant Pot Rava Idli Sabbakki

Cook Time: 12 minutes

Servings: 15

Ingredients:

- 1 cup of semolina (sooji)
- 1 tablespoon of mustard seeds
- 1 teaspoon of cumin seeds
- 1 tablespoon of Chana dal

- 1 tablespoon of split black dal
- 1/3 cup of sliced cashew nuts
- 1 sprig of shredded curry leaves
- 1 tablespoon of grated ginger
- Asafoetida to taste
- 2 green chilies, chopped
- Oil as needed
- 2 tablespoons of thinly sliced coriander leaves
- Salt to taste
- ¼ cup of tapioca pearls
- 1 cup of beaten yogurt
- Oil for greasing

Instructions:

1. Soak tapioca pearls in water for two hours. Drain excess water using fingertips; slight crumbling is okay.
2. Roast semolina until golden. Add dals, curry leaves, ginger, and chilies; cook for 5 minutes until well-cooked.
3. Combine semolina mixture, drained tapioca pearls, coriander, salt, and yogurt; blend well.
4. Pour the batter into idli molds and steam for 15 minutes. Serve hot.

❖ Instant Pot Rotli's Vaghareli

Servings: 2

Cooking Time: 30 minute

Ingredients:

- 4 or 5 leftover chapattis
- One cup of yogurt
- Two teaspoons of minced garlic
- One spoonful of mustard seeds
- Two crushed green chilies
- One tablespoon of turmeric
- One spoonful of cooking oil
- Salt to taste
- A handful of cilantro
- One tablespoon of lemon juice

Instructions:

1. Break chapattis into pieces.
2. Turn on sauté mode. Heat oil, add seeds, and cook for 3 minutes.
3. Add chapatti pieces and mix well.
4. Add all the ingredients, stir, and cook for 5-7 minutes until chapattis absorb the liquid.
5. Turn off the Instant Pot and serve.

❖ Instant Pot Pohe Tomato with Peas

Cooking Time: 50 minutes

Servings: 3

Ingredients:

- Two teaspoons of olive oil
- One large onion, minced
- One clove of garlic, thinly sliced
- Three small tomatoes, thinly sliced
- ½ cup of sugar
- One teaspoon of fresh oregano
- 1 cup of water (or as needed)
- One teaspoon of tomato paste
- One small diced zucchini
- 1 cup of peas
- Salt to taste

Instructions:

1. Soak poha in water for 10 minutes; drain thoroughly.
2. Turn on sauté mode. Add all ingredients and stir.
3. Seal the Instant Pot, set the pressure valve to sealing, and pressure cook for 5 minutes.
4. Transfer to a serving bowl, garnish with coriander, and serve immediately.

❖ Dadpe Pohe

Servings: 3

Cooking Time: 30 minutes

Ingredients:

- 1 ½ cups of small flattened rice
- 1 cup of thinly sliced onion
- ¾ cup of grated coconut
- 4 teaspoons of powdered sugar
- 2 teaspoons of lemon zest
- Fresh peanuts to taste
- Coriander for garnish (optional)
- Salt to taste
- Two tablespoons of oil
- ¼ teaspoon of asafetida

Instructions:

1. Combine finely sliced onions, grated coconut, cinnamon, sugar, lemon zest, and rice in a bowl.
2. Heat oil in the Instant Pot using sauté mode. Add fresh peanuts and fry until brown. Remove and set aside.
3. In the same oil, add mustard seeds, asafetida, chopped chilies, curry leaves, and spices.
4. Add the rice mixture and quickly toss everything.
5. Seal the Instant Pot, set the pressure valve to sealing, and pressure cook for 5 minutes.
6. Serve this flavorful Dadpe Pohe for breakfast or brunch.

❖ Dosa Aval

Cooking Time: 20 minutes
Servings: 4

Ingredients:

- Three cups of rice
- Two cups of dal
- Two teaspoons of fenugreek seeds
- Salt and pepper to taste
- Oil as needed
- Water as required

Instructions:

1. Rinse rice and dal separately in running water and soak them in containers with salted water.
2. Let the rice and dal soak for at least 6 hours or overnight.
3. Wash Aval (flattened rice) and add it to the soaked rice.
4. Grind the dal, rice mixture, and fenugreek seeds in a grinder until smooth.
5. Transfer the overnight batter to a bowl.
6. Seal the Instant Pot, set the pressure valve to sealing, and pressure cook for 5-7 minutes.
7. Add salt to the batter.
8. Heat a Dosa Tawa and pour a ladle of dosa batter.
9. Spread it evenly with a slotted spoon. Drizzle some oil around the edges.
10. Cook until it turns golden brown.

Enjoy crispy and delicious Dosa Aval, perfect for a delightful meal!

❖ Instant Pot Foxtail Millet

Cooking Time: 10 minutes
Servings: 3

Ingredients:

- 3 cups of foxtail millet
- 1 cup of daal
- 1 tablespoon of fenugreek seeds
- Oil as needed
- Water as needed
- Salt to taste

Instructions:

1. Soak the millet and Urad Dal separately in water for 6 hours, along with the immersed Fenugreek seeds.
2. Grind the millet and Dal separately.
3. Blend the soaked dal and Fenugreek seeds into a fine paste. Transfer it to a bowl. Then, grind the soaked millet in the same blender and add it to the Dal batter.
4. Mix the batter well and let it ferment overnight. Stir well after fermenting.
5. Add salt and adjust the consistency with water for making idli batter. Grease the idli plate with butter, then steam it in the instant pot for 10 minutes in sauté mode.
6. Allow it to cool slightly, then sprinkle with water and remove the hot Idli.

7. To prepare dosa, add water to the batter to reach the desired consistency. Heat a dosa tawa, pour a spoonful of batter, and spread it evenly. Cook, and drizzle oil around the edges.
8. Flip to the other side, fry, and then serve.

❖ Instant Pot Dosa Rava Onion

Cooking Time: 15 minutes

Servings: 3

Ingredients:

- ½ cup of semolina
- 2 teaspoons sliced coriander
- One sprig stripped curry leaves
- ½ cup of rice flour
- One tablespoon roughly minced ginger
- One sliced chili
- ¼ cup of Maida
- One teaspoon cumin seeds
- One thinly sliced onion
- Ghee, as needed

Instructions:

1. Combine all ingredients in a bowl except onions, and add water. Use a whisk for quick mixing.
2. Set aside the onions. The batter should be thin.

3. Heat a non-stick dosa plate. Drizzle and spread the soupy batter with some grease, first creating a larger ring and then filling in the middle.
4. Immediately sprinkle the sliced onions on top. Add a teaspoon of oil/ghee. Cook over medium flame until the dosa turns golden brown.
5. Serve hot.

❖ Instant Pot Dosa Buckwheat

Servings: 10
Cooking Time: 10 minutes

Ingredients:

- 1 cup of buckwheat flour
- ½ cup of oat flour
- ½ cup of almond flour
- Water, as needed
- ½ teaspoon of salt
- Oil for greasing

Instructions:

1. Whisk buckwheat, oat, and almond flours together to prepare a smooth batter. Cover and let it sit at room temperature in the refrigerator overnight to soften.
2. Add water and mix well.
3. Turn on the sauté mode of the instant pot.
4. Grease it with a thin layer of oil. Pour a spoonful of batter onto it.

5. Cook for 3 minutes. Flip it to the other side.
6. Serve hot.

❖ Instant Pot Dosa Dhania Palak

Cooking Time: 10 minutes

Servings: 5

Ingredients:

- 2 ½ cups of rice, soaked overnight
- 1 cup of dal, soaked overnight
- One tablespoon of fenugreek seeds
- Salt to taste
- Spinach and coriander leaves, finely chopped
- Oil for cooking

Instructions:

1. Wash the rice, spinach, and coriander leaves thoroughly in water. Ensure the rice is completely submerged.
2. Let the dal soak for about six hours.
3. The batter should appear fluffy. Transfer this batter into a bowl.
4. Using too much water will make the dosa mixture too watery. The rice batter can be a little thicker, but it must be extremely soft for the dal batter.
5. Mix the vegetables and the batter together. In sauté mode, take a handful of batter and drop it into the center of the pot. Spread it uniformly in

a clockwise direction toward the outside. Cook until it's golden brown, then serve.

❖ Instant Pot Ragi Rava Idli

Servings: 4

Cooking Time: 20 minutes

Ingredients:

- 1 cup of idli rice
- 2 cups of flour
- 1 cup of dal
- ½ teaspoon of fenugreek seeds
- Salt to taste

Instructions:

1. Wash and soak fenugreek seeds, urad dal, and fenugreek for 4 hours. Clean and rinse rice separately for 5 hours.
2. Blend dal and seeds until smooth and creamy. Transfer to a container and set aside.
3. Grind rice to a coarse flour, add water to create a visibly rough mixture or batter.
4. Mix rice batter into the dal-seed mixture. Add salt and other spices, and blend until well combined.
5. Allow it to rest. Use a wide vessel to prevent spills since it can double in volume during fermentation.

6. The batter for Ragi Idli is ready.
7. Turn on the sauté mode. Boil water in it for a while. Spoon the idli mixture into it.
8. Cook for 20 minutes or until a toothpick inserted into the idli comes out clean.
9. Serve the hot Ragi Idli with your choice of chutney.

❖ Instant Pot Tamarind and Rava Upma Rice

Cooking Time: 20-30 minutes

Serves: 6-8

Ingredients:

- 2 cups of Rava rice
- One thinly chopped onion
- 3-4 green chilies, chopped
- ½ roughly chopped ginger
- 1 cup of minced vegetables
- 1 ½ teaspoons of ghee
- Nine cashew nuts (optional)
- 4 cups of water
- Salt

For Seasoning:

- One teaspoon of mustard seeds
- One sprig of curry leaves
- One teaspoon of cumin seeds
- One teaspoon of Bengal gram
- One teaspoon of black gram

Instructions:

1. Wash and soak rice, spinach, and coriander leaves in water. Ensure the rice is fully submerged.
2. Let the dal simmer for about six hours.
3. The batter should be fluffy. Transfer this batter into a bowl.
4. Using too

much water will make the dosa mixture too watery. The rice batter can be a little thicker, but it must be extremely soft for the dal batter.

5. Mix the vegetables and the batter together. In sauté mode, take a handful of batter and drop it into the center of the pot. Spread it uniformly in a clockwise direction toward the outside. Cook until it's golden brown, then serve.

3

Chapter 02: Instant Pot Indian Lunch & Dinner Recipes****

In this section, we explore hearty lunch and dinner options, emphasizing that while a light dinner might suffice, a substantial lunch can enhance your day. The chapter provides an array of recipes tailored for both lunch and dinner settings. Beyond the recipes, it aims to inspire creativity, encouraging you to experiment with the presented ideas or invent your own dishes not mentioned here.

❖ Instant Pot Chicken Biryani

Cooking Time: 1 hour 40 minutes
Servings: 4

Ingredients:

- 1 ½ cups of rice
- Water as needed
- 10 ounces of chicken breast, cut into 1-inch cubes
- Three tablespoons of yogurt
- Two teaspoons of lime zest
- ½ tablespoon of minced ginger and garlic
- ½ tablespoon of garam masala
- Salt, red chili, and pepper to taste
- Ghee as needed
- Two cloves
- One bay leaf
- Half stick of cinnamon
- One teaspoon of coriander
- One teaspoon of mustard seeds
- One large red onion, diced
- 1 cup of chicken broth
- ½ cup of minced cilantro
- ½ teaspoon of turmeric powder

Instructions:

1. Rinse the rice thoroughly in a strainer. Transfer the rice to a bowl, add clean water, and let it soak for 40 minutes.
2. In a large bowl, combine chicken pieces with yogurt, lime zest, ginger, garlic, cinnamon, garam masala, and pepper. Rub the mixture onto the chicken evenly. Allow it to marinate for 30 minutes.
3. Preheat the Instant Pot using the sauté button. Add oil and let it heat. Stir in all the remaining ingredients and sauté for 5-8 minutes.
4. Add the marinated chicken and cook until it browns.
5. Turn off the sauté function. Add rice, broth, and spices. Mix well.

6. Seal the instant pot, set the pressure valve to sealing position, and cook on pressure cooker mode for 5-7 minutes.
7. Turn off the pot and serve with yogurt.

❖ Instant Pot Chicken Tikka Masala

Servings: 4

Cooking Time: 3 hours

Ingredients:

- Eight chicken bone-in thighs
- 1 tablespoon lime zest
- For Marinade:
- Ginger, mashed
- Ten cloves of garlic, mashed
- Yogurt as needed
- A pinch of chili powder
- One teaspoon of coriander
- One teaspoon of cumin
- One teaspoon of garam masala
- One teaspoon of turmeric
- One small chili
- For the Sauce:
- 1 ½ tablespoons of butter
- One large onion, coarsely diced
- One tablespoon of cumin seeds
- One tablespoon of mustard seeds
- ½ teaspoon of crushed fenugreek

- ½ teaspoon of paprika
- Three cardamom pods
- One large cinnamon stick
- One tablespoon of tomato purée
- One teaspoon of vinegar
- Milk as needed

Instructions: [Instructions for Chicken Tikka Masala were not provided in the original text. Please provide specific instructions if needed.]

Instant Pot Indian Masala Pasta

Servings: 3
Cooking Time: 1 hour

Ingredients:

- 1 cup of pasta (choose your favorite)
- 1 tablespoon of olive oil
- 1 teaspoon of cumin seeds
- Three cloves of sliced garlic
- Three small sliced onions
- 3 thin, diced tomatoes
- 1 tablespoon of turmeric powder
- 1 teaspoon of curry powder (optional)
- 1 tablespoon of coriander powder
- Ground red chili to taste
- Salt to taste
- 1 cup of water, or as needed

Instructions:

1. Heat your Instant Pot using the high sauté mode. Add oil and let it warm up.
2. Add garlic, onions, and cumin seeds. Sauté for a while.
3. Add tomatoes and cook until tender. Add all the dried spices and salt.
4. Sauté for one or two minutes.
5. Add pasta and water. Mix thoroughly, then turn off sauté mode.
6. Set it to high pressure for 7 minutes, ensuring the vent is sealed. After 10 minutes, release the pressure.
7. Serve as desired.

Instant Pot Garlic Mushrooms

Servings: 3
Cooking Time: 1 hour

Ingredients:

- Two tablespoons of butter
- 2 tablespoons of oil
- Quarter cup of finely sliced onion
- 1 cup of Button Mushrooms, sliced
- Two tablespoons of finely minced garlic
- Two tablespoons of thinly sliced fresh parsley
- ½ teaspoon of finely minced thyme
- ½ tablespoon of finely chopped fresh oregano
- Red chili flakes to taste

Instructions:

1. Turn on the sauté mode of the Instant Pot. Add oil.
2. Add onions and sauté for 3 minutes.
3. Add all the ingredients. Let it cook for 10 minutes.
4. Add the rest of the parsley and turn off the sauté button.
5. Serve as desired.

Instant Pot Makhni Dal

Servings: 4
Cooking Time: 2 hours

Ingredients:

- Two teaspoons of red beans, soaked overnight
- 1 spoonful of red chili powder
- Eight teaspoons of butter
- One tall onion, chopped
- Half cup of tomato puree
- Half cup of fresh milk
- Half teaspoon of ginger paste
- Salt to taste
- Two slices of ginger, diced
- Two large green chilies, diced
- ½ cup of dal, soaked overnight
- 1/2 teaspoon of garlic paste

Instructions:

1. Soak dal overnight in two cups of water. Drain it, then cook it in the Instant Pot with salt and 3 cups of water until tender.
2. Turn on the sauté mode. Add all the spices and other ingredients except Rajma and Dal. Let it cook for 10 minutes.
3. When the masala is to your liking, add Rajma and dal, and let it simmer. If the dal is too thick, add more water.

Instant Pot Pickle Chicken

Servings: 4

Cooking Time: 2 hours

Ingredients:

- Four skinless chicken breasts
- 1 tablespoon of pickle
- 1 tablespoon of honey
- 1 cup of oil
- Two cloves of minced garlic
- 1 teaspoon of crushed oregano
- Fresh green salad and potatoes for serving

Instructions:

1. Preheat the Instant Pot using the oven mode. Grease it with oil. Place chicken in it.
2. In a separate pan, combine all the other ingredients and cook for 5 minutes. Pour the mixture over the chicken.
3. Close the lid and grill the chicken for 45 minutes.
4. Let the chicken cool for 5 minutes before serving with a green salad and fresh potatoes.

Instant Pot Fried Chettinad Trout

Servings: 2
Cooking Time: 2 hours

Ingredients:

- 400g fish
- 1 tablespoon of turmeric powder
- Salt, pepper, and chili to taste
- One tablespoon of lime zest
- Three onions, chopped
- 2 garlic cloves, diced
- Two tablespoons of minced ginger
- Two teaspoons of Cumin seeds
- Two teaspoons of rice flour
- Oil as needed
- One tablespoon of coriander powder

Instructions:

1. Marinate the fish.
2. Blend cumin seeds, garlic, ginger, and onion in a blender.
3. Coat the fish with the paste.
4. Heat oil. Fry the fish on one side until cooked, then turn it over.

Instant Pot Oats Cheela with Stuffed Palak

Cooking Time: 40 minutes

Serving: 4

Ingredients:

- 1 cup of gram flour
- 2 to 3 teaspoons of oil
- ¼ teaspoon of carom seeds
- ¼ teaspoon of red chili powder
- 1 cup of thinly sliced spinach
- Salt to taste

Instructions:

10) Begin by preparing the besan cheela batter and take a spoonful of it.

11) Pour the batter into the Instant Pot with hot oil.

12) Ensure all sides of the cheela are well-cooked.

13) Serve it.

Instant Pot Chicken Curry Mango

Serves: 4

Cooking Time: 2 hours

Ingredients:

- Two teaspoons of coconut oil
- One large sliced onion
- Four cloves of garlic
- Eight teaspoons of chopped ginger
- Four teaspoons of curry powder
- Salt and pepper, to taste
- 3 sliced, diced, and peeled mangos
- Coconut milk, as needed
- 2-4 Chicken thighs, sliced

Instructions:

1. Switch on the Instant Pot's sauté mode. Heat coconut oil in it. Add onions, garlic, and ginger; cook until brown.
2. Add curry powder, salt, pepper, 1 cup of fresh mangoes, and coconut milk. Mix well.
3. Pour the sauce into the pot, add chicken and 1/2 cup of water. Cover and cook for 20 minutes.
4. Serve when the chicken pieces are thoroughly cooked.

Instant Pot Tandoori Curry Sandwich

Serves: 4

Cooking Time: 1 hour

Ingredients:

- One whole chicken, cut into pieces
- 1 cup Greek yogurt
- ½ yellow onion, diced
- One peeled, freshly grated ginger
- Two garlic cloves
- Two tablespoons fresh citrus juice
- ½ teaspoon cumin
- ½ teaspoon ground cilantro
- One tablespoon olive oil
- Salt and potatoes

For Making Sandwiches:

- Big, half-warmed whole wheat bread
- Regular yogurt
- ½ teaspoon cumin powder
- ½ teaspoon ground cilantro
- ¼ teaspoon garlic powder
- Salt and tomatoes
- Lettuce

Instructions:

1. Marinate the chicken.
2. Preheat the Instant Pot using the oven mode. Put the chicken in it, skin-side down. Roast for about 35 minutes, tossing once.
3. In a shallow bowl, blend yogurt and spices. Fill bread slices with chicken, lettuce, sauce, and yogurt.
4. Serve as desired.

Instant Pot Butter and Chicken Curry

Serves: 3

Cooking Time: 2 hours

Ingredients:

- Two tablespoons butter
- One large white onion, finely diced
- 2 large garlic cloves
- One teaspoon fresh ginger
- One tablespoon Garam Masala
- One tablespoon curry powder
- One tablespoon cilantro powder
- ½ teaspoon paprika
- ¼ teaspoon cinnamon
- ¼ teaspoon chili flakes
- Two tomatoes
- 400 ml coconut milk

Instructions:

1. Add onion to the Instant Pot and sauté for about 6 minutes or until translucent.
2. Add ginger and sauté for 5 minutes until aromatic. Add Garam Masala, curry powder, cilantro, paprika, and cinnamon.
3. Return the sauce to the pot. Add cooked lentils, tomatoes, chickpeas, and vegan chicken. Cook for 10-15 minutes.

Instant Pot Lime Chicken

Serves: 4
Cooking Time: 2 hours

Ingredients:

- Four skinless chicken breasts
- One tablespoon lemon zest
- One tablespoon honey
- 1 cup oil
- Two cloves of minced garlic
- One teaspoon crushed oregano
- Fresh green salad and potatoes, for serving

Instructions:

1. Preheat the gas oven to 170C. Place the chicken in a deep oven tray in a single layer.
2. In a pan, combine all the ingredients and heat for 1 minute or until warm. Pour over the chicken.
3. Grill the chicken for 45 minutes, basting every 10 minutes. The juices will gradually thicken, giving the chicken a glossy coating.
4. Let the chicken rest for 5 minutes before serving with a green salad and fresh potatoes.

Instant Pot Spicy Beef Curry Stew

Cooking Time: 1 hour 40 minutes
Servings: 7

Ingredients:

- One tablespoon Olive oil
- 2 pounds of cubed beef stew
- Salt and black pepper, to taste
- Two jalapeno peppers, sliced
- Four minced garlic cloves
- One tablespoon minced ginger
- Eight teaspoons curry powder
- 2 cups beef broth
- One diced tomato
- One pound chopped potatoes
- One large chopped onion

Instructions:

1. Turn on the Instant Pot's sauté mode. Add olive oil and cook for 2 minutes. Add jalapenos, garlic, and ginger. Cook for about 3 minutes or until soft. Season with curry powder.
2. Choose high pressure as per the manufacturer's instructions and set the timer for 30 minutes. Allow pressure to build for 15 minutes.

Instant Pot Khichdi

Cooking Time: 45 minutes
Servings: 6

Ingredients:

1. Wash basmati rice and yellow lentils in water for 15-30 minutes. Drain, then set aside.
2. Click the sauté button, then add ghee. Let it warm up for a minute, then add seeds, bay leaf, rice, lentils, six cups of water, and spices.
3. Close the lid, turn on the pressure valve. Cook at high pressure for 25 minutes.

Instant Pot Madras Curry Chicken

Serves: 4
Cooking Time: 2 hours

Ingredients:

- Ghee
  - Onion
  - Coriander
  - Garlic
  - Fresh ginger
  - Salt, to taste
  - Boneless chicken thighs

, skinless
  - Citrus zest
  - Finely sliced tomatoes
  - Curry Powder
  - Coconut milk

Instructions:

1. Turn on the Instant Pot's sauté mode. Add sliced onion, chopped garlic, and smashed ginger to the oil. Sauté for 10 minutes until onions are very tender.
2. Add curry powder, salt, and chili powder. Cook until aromatic.
3. Increase the heat to normal, add coconut milk and tomatoes. Cook for a while.
4. Add sliced chicken into the gravy. Cover and cook, stirring frequently, for 25 minutes.

Instant Pot Beef Kofta with Spinach and Potatoes

Serves: 4
Cooking Time: 1 hour

Ingredients:

- One onion
- One garlic clove
- Two small-medium potatoes
- ½ bunch of coriander
- ½ teaspoon cumin
- ½ teaspoon turmeric
- ½ teaspoon mustard
- Chicken reserve (one pot)
- 300 g of minced beef
- Coconut Milk, as needed
- ½ teaspoon lemon zest
- Water

Instructions:

1. Turn on the Instant Pot's sauté mode. Add garlic and onion; sauté for 5 minutes or until tender. Keep half of this aside and set aside in a tray.
2. Close the lid and let it cook for 10 minutes.
3. Meanwhile, place beef in a bowl and mix with salt, black pepper, and grind.
4. Form the mixture into koftas and gently boil them in the boiling mixture.
5. Add spinach. Cook for a while.

Instant Pot Indian Koftey

Serves: 3

Cooking Time: 2 hours

Ingredients:

- 400g Indian Cottage Cheese
- 2 big baked and mashed potatoes
- 2 chopped Green Chilies
- 1/4 teaspoon white pepper powder
- Two broad tablespoons of cornflour
- 4 tablespoons of oil
- Salt, to taste

For the gravy preparation:

- A quarter cup of oil
- 2 moderate sliced onions
- One tablespoon of ginger
- Half a garlic plant, sliced
- 20 cashews, soaked for 10 minutes
- 1 cup pureed tomatoes
- 1 dark cardamom
- 3 gray cardamom
- One Bay leaf
- One pinch of cinnamon
- Half a teaspoon of chili powder
- 2 teaspoons of milk
- One teaspoon Kasuri methi (fenugreek)
- Salt, to taste

Instructions:

1. Combine all the ingredients well and form them into balls (excluding the oil).
2. Heat oil in the pot and fry the Koftas until both sides are golden brown.
3. In a processor, blend the remaining onions, ginger, garlic, and cashews into a fine paste.
4. Put tomato puree, Kashmiri red chili, and salt in the clean pot. Add a glass of water and cook on a moderate flame for 20 minutes.
5. Put the sauce into a deep bowl. One by one, gently lower the koftas into the sauce, ensuring not to stack them on top of each other.

4

Chapter 03: Instant Pot Vegetarian Dishes

In today's health-conscious era, an increasing number of individuals are leaning towards vegetarian cuisine, eschewing non-vegetarian options due to concerns about elevated fat content and sluggish digestion linked to various health conditions like obesity, thyroid issues, and weight gain. Within this chapter, you'll explore a variety of vegetarian dishes that not only satiate your taste buds but also offer substantial nutrition.

❖ Instant Pot Vegetable Biryani

Serving Size: 3 persons
Cooking Time: 2 hours

Ingredients:

- 2 teaspoons of oil
- Small cauliflower, divided into small florets
- 2 large sweet potatoes, peeled and cubed
- 1 large onion, chopped
- Bunch of hot veggies
- 1 tablespoon of curry paste
- 1 chili, thinly sliced
- Large pinch of saffron threads
- 1 tablespoon of mustard seeds
- 500g Rice
- 140g beans
- 2 tablespoons of lemon juice
- Handful of coriander leaves

Instructions:

1. Activate the sauté mode on the Instant Pot. Heat oil, add onions, and sauté until softened. Mix in cumin seeds and cook until they start popping.
2. Add ginger-garlic paste, onions, and sugar paste. Boil until water is absorbed. Add peas, onions, carrots, and spices. Stir, cover, and simmer for three minutes.
3. Pour in water and rice. Seal the Instant Pot, set to pressure cook for 5-7 minutes.
4. Release pressure following instructions.
5. Serve.

❖ Instant Pot Paneer Crepes and Green Peas

Cooking Time: 45 minutes

Serving Size: 4 persons

Ingredients:

- 1 cup Green peas
- 2 cups Paneer (Homemade Cottage Cheese)
- 2 tablespoons chopped Ginger
- 2 Green Chilies, sliced
- 2 teaspoons Turmeric powder
- 4 teaspoons Red Chili Powder
- 2 teaspoons Amchur
- 2 teaspoons Powdered Coriander
- 1 cup wheat flour
- Olive oil for kneading

Instructions:

1. Drizzle oil on the dough, knead. Add cumin seeds.
2. Cook crushed paneer until spices blend. Roll out dough, add filling, seal, and cook on Instant Pot.
3. Drizzle ghee, cook until golden brown.

❖ Instant Pot Indian Sparkling Dhal

Serving Size: 4 persons

Cooking Time: 1 hour

Ingredients:

- 1 tablespoon of oil
- 1 cup sliced onion
- 2 cloves garlic, thinly sliced
- 1 tablespoon coarsely diced ginger
- 4 cups water
- 1 cup rinsed dried red lentils
- 1 tablespoon cumin
- 1 tablespoon coriander
- 1 tablespoon turmeric
- 1/4 teaspoon cardamom
- 1/4 teaspoon cinnamon
- 1/4 teaspoon pepper
- Salt to taste
- 2 tablespoons tomato paste

Instructions:

1. Heat oil in Instant Pot. Add onion, garlic, and ginger. Cook for 6 minutes.
2. Add water, lentils, vegetables, and salt. Bring to a boil, then pressure cook for 5-7 minutes.
3. Serve.

❖ Instant Pot Koora Cabbage

Serving Size: 4 persons

Cooking Time: 2 hours

Ingredients:

- 3 tablespoons cooking oil
- 2 dried hot chili peppers, chopped
- 1 tablespoon black split skinned lentils
- 1 tablespoon Bengal gram
- 1 teaspoon mustard seeds
- Curry leaves
- Pinch of Asafetida powder
- 4 green chili peppers, chopped
- Thinly sliced cabbage
- 1/4 cup frozen peas
- Coconut

Instructions:

1. Heat oil in Instant Pot. Cook peppers, lentils, and mustard until golden. Add curry leaves and asafetida.
2. Add green chilies, cabbage, peas, and lentils. Season, cook until wilted but slightly crunchy, about 10 minutes.
3. Add coconut, simmer 2 minutes.
4. Serve immediately.

❖ Instant Pot Indian Dhal with Spinach

Serving Size: 4 persons

Cooking Time: 2 hours

Ingredients:

- 2 cups yellow split peas
- 8 cups water
- 2 teaspoons lemon juice
- 2 teaspoons kosher salt
- 8 teaspoons unsalted butter
- 2 teaspoons cumin seeds
- 1 ½ teaspoons turmeric
- 5 garlic cloves, minced
- ¼ cup fresh ginger, finely chopped
- 1 medium serrano chili, thinly sliced
- 8 ounces spinach, coarsely chopped

Instructions:

1. Simmer peas until soft, thickening soup for 30 minutes.
2. Add cumin seeds and turmeric, toast for 3 minutes.
3. Add spinach, wilt for 4 minutes.

❖ Instant Pot Masor Daal

Serving Size: 4 persons
Cooking Time: 2 hours

Ingredients:

- 2 cups dry Masor dal, rinsed
- 8 cups water
- 1 tablespoon flavored coconut oil

- 1 large yellow onion, finely diced
- 6 cloves garlic, minced
- 1 tablespoon minced ginger
- 2 green chilies, minced
- 1 tablespoon Indian curry powder
- 1 teaspoon whole seed mustard
- 1 teaspoon coriander
- ½ teaspoon cumin
- 1 ½ teaspoon salt
- 1 ½ cups chopped tomatoes

Instructions:

1. Mix lentils and water in Instant Pot.
2. Add spices, salt, curry powder, mustard, coriander, cumin, and tomatoes. Pressure cook for 60 seconds.
3. Add tadka, simmer 5 minutes.

❖ Instant Pot Indian Eggplant

Cooking Time: 1 hour 40 minutes
Servings: 4

Ingredients:

- 2 eggplants
- 2 tablespoons vegetable oil
- 1 teaspoon curry powder
- 1 teaspoon ground cumin
- ½ teaspoon turmeric

- Thinly sliced onion
- 2 teaspoons diced ginger
- 1 tablespoon diced garlic
- 3 tomatoes, diced
- Salt and pepper to taste
- 1 cup defrosted peas

Instructions:

1. Place eggplant on Instant Pot rack with 1 cup of water. Sauté oil, tomatoes, and spices. Add peas and eggplant, simmer for 2-3 minutes.

❖ Instant Pot Indian Chickpeas

Cooking Time: 60 minutes

Servings: 4

Ingredients:

- 2 cups chickpeas
- 4 cups water
- Salt and pepper to taste

Instructions:

1. Soak chickpeas for 7 hours, simmer in 2 cups water. In Instant Pot, add chickpeas, water, and salt. Pressure cook for 30 minutes.

❖ Instant Pot Indian Okra

Cooking Time: 20 minutes

Servings: 2

Ingredients:

- 1 tablespoon oil
- ¼ tablespoon cumin seeds
- 3 cloves garlic, finely diced
- 1 onion, diced
- 1 tomato, diced
- 1 pound okra,

sliced

- ¼ tablespoon turmeric
- ½ tablespoon powdered coriander
- Salt, pepper, and red chili to taste

Instructions:

1. In sauté mode, warm Instant Pot, add oil. After 2 minutes, add ingredients except okra.
2. Cook 5 minutes. Add okra, pressure cook for 5 minutes.
3. Release pressure, swirl okra, serve.

Instant Pot Bhel Puri

Servings: 3
Cooking Time: 30 minutes

Ingredients:

- 2 cups puffed rice
- 1/4 cup chopped onions
- 1/4 cup diced tomatoes
- 1 tablespoon chutney (of your choice)
- 1 tablespoon mint chutney
- Masala spices to taste

Instructions:

1. Combine onions, peas, and chutney in a bowl. Let it sit for a few minutes to meld the flavors.
2. In the Instant Pot, sauté puffed rice for about 1 minute. Do not overcook, as it may lose its crunch.
3. Quickly mix the puffed rice into the mixture; it should be done swiftly to preserve the crunch.
4. Garnish with masala spices.

Instant Pot Spicy Corn Salad

Servings: 4 cups
Cooking Time: 15 minutes

Ingredients:

- 3 cups corn
- 2 tablespoons mayonnaise
- 1 tablespoon lime zest
- 1 small onion, finely chopped
- 2 teaspoons crumbled fresco cheese
- Salt and pepper to taste
- Lime wedges for garnish

Instructions:

1. Sauté corn in Instant Pot using sauté mode.
2. In a large bowl, mix onion, mayonnaise, chili lime sauce, and lemon zest thoroughly using a fork.
3. Add cooked corn to the mixture.
4. Serve in cups, garnished with minced lime wedges.

Instant Pot Idli Chaat

Cooking Time: 30 minutes
Servings:4

Ingredients:

- 3 cups Idli rice (soaked for 5-6 hours)
- 1 cup whole black lentils without skin (soaked for 5-6 hours)
- 1 teaspoon fenugreek seeds (soaked for 5-6 hours)
- 2 cups water
- Salt and pepper to taste

Instructions:

1. Blend drained rice with 1 cup of water until creamy.
2. In the same processor, add drained lentils and seeds, pouring the remaining 1 cup of water slowly while grinding.
3. Combine rice and lentils mixture.
4. Let the batter rise until doubled in size, then gently fold in salt.

5. Use the batter for idlis in the first two days and for crispy dosas for the rest of the week.

Instant Pot Dosa Rava Onion

Cooking Time: 15 minutes
Servings: 3 persons

Ingredients:

- ½ cup semolina (sooji)
- 2 teaspoons sliced coriander
- 1 sprig curry leaves, stripped
- ½ cup rice flour
- 1 tablespoon minced ginger
- 1 sliced chili
- ¼ cup Maida
- 1 teaspoon cumin seeds
- 1 thinly sliced onion
- Ghee, as needed

Instructions:

1. Mix all ingredients except onions in a bowl. Add water.
2. Heat the pot and ladle the batter, creating a larger ring first and then filling in the middle.
3. Immediately sprinkle sliced onions on top, drizzle with a teaspoon of oil. Cook until golden brown.

4. Serve hot.

Instant Pot Palak Pulao

Servings: 4
Cooking Time: 45 minutes

Ingredients:

- 1 cup rice
- 1 diced onion
- Salt and pepper to taste
- 1/4 cup peas
- 2 medium-sized potatoes, cubed
- 1 cup water
- 2 cups roughly chopped spinach
- 2 green chilis, roughly chopped
- 2 cloves garlic and ginger
- 2 teaspoons ghee
- Bay leaf
- Cinnamon
- 1/2 tablespoon cumin seeds

Instructions:

1. Add spices and ghee. Stir in blended paste, then add remaining vegetables.
2. Add rice, salt, and water.
3. Carefully open the lid and serve hot.

Instant Cucumber Tomato Corn Peanut Salad

Servings: 4
Cooking Time: 30 minutes

Ingredients:

- 1 cucumber, chopped
- 1 tomato, chopped
- 1 onion, chopped
- ½ cup boiled sweet corn
- 1 green chili, sliced
- 1 tablespoon roasted peanuts
- 1 teaspoon lime zest
- Salt and pepper to taste
- 2 sprigs coriander

Instructions:

1. Sauté corn kernels in Instant Pot with water for 7 minutes.
2. Drain corn. Mix cucumber, pepper, cabbage, corn, green chili, and peanuts in a bowl.
3. Squeeze lime juice, add salt, and mix.
4. Garnish with coriander.

Instant Pot Bengali Vegetable Form Pohe

Cooking Time: 40 minutes

Ingredients:

- ½ cup Maida
- ½ cup semolina (sooji)
- 1 tablespoon sugar
- 1 tablespoon shredded fennel seeds
- 350ml evaporated milk
- Oil for frying
- 1 cup drinking water
- 4 green cardamom
- 1 cup sugar

Instructions:

1. Mix all batter ingredients in a bowl until smooth.
2. Heat oil for deep frying. Shape small pancakes, spoon a bit of batter into hot oil.
3. Fry until golden brown, then soak in sugar syrup immediately.

Instant Pot Sesame and Beetroot Thepla

Cooking Time: 25 minutes
Servings: 2 persons

Ingredients:

- 1 grated beetroot
- ½ cup ground wheat
- ½ cup besan
- ½ teaspoon cumin powder
- ½ teaspoon Amchur
- ½ teaspoon Garam masala powder
- 1 teaspoon red chili powder
- Oil, as needed
- Salt, to taste

Instructions:

1. Combine all ingredients, including salt and ghee, with grated beetroot.
2. Shape a small portion into a thepla.
3. Cook for about a minute on one side, flip, and cook for another minute.

Instant Pot Apple Chutney

Servings: 10 persons

Cooking Time: 20 minutes

Ingredients:

- 1 tablespoon oil
- ½ teaspoon cumin seeds
- ½ teaspoon fennel seeds

- ½ teaspoon fenugreek seeds
- ½ teaspoon mustard seeds
- Curry leaves
- 4 apples, cubed
- ½ tablespoon turmeric
- ½ tablespoon ginger powder
- Salt and pepper to taste
- 3 tablespoons cider vinegar
- 3 tablespoons sugar

Instructions:

1. Heat oil in sauté mode. Add seeds and curry leaves.
2. Add apples and spices; cook until seeds begin to brown, about 5 minutes.
3. Blend the mixture into a puree using a processor.
4. Store in an airtight jar in the fridge for up to one week or in the freezer for up to one month.

Instant Pot Spicy Lime Pickle

Servings: 12 servings

Cooking Time: 1 hour

Ingredients:

- 6 medium-sized lemons
-

1 teaspoon black mustard seeds
- 1 teaspoon fenugreek seeds
- 1 teaspoon fennel seeds
- 2 tablespoons olive oil
- 1 teaspoon black mustard
- Salt and red chili powder to taste

Instructions:

Instant Pot Steamed Broccoli

Servings: 4
Cooking Time: 10 minutes

Ingredients:

- 2 heads of broccoli
- 1 cup of water
- Salt and pepper to taste
- Two teaspoons of olive oil

Instructions:

1. Rinse and chop the broccoli into florets.
2. Place the steamer rack in the Instant Pot and pour a cup of water into the pot. Add broccoli and salt.
3. Close the lid, lock it in place, and set the vent to sealing position. Press the pressure cook button and set the timer to 3 minutes.
4. Manually release the pressure. Wait until the pin drops and the pot

unlocks.

5. Season the broccoli with salt, pepper, and olive oil.
6. Serve immediately.

5

Chapter 04: Instant Pot Indian Snacks Recipes

When hunger strikes lightly and a heavy meal isn't what you're after, snacks are the perfect solution. They are not only easy to prepare but can be enjoyed at any time. In this chapter, discover a variety of Indian snack recipes that can be effortlessly made in the Instant Pot.

❖ Instant Pot Chana Masala

Cooking Time: 5 hours*
Servings: 5

Ingredients:

- 1 cup dry chickpeas (rinsed)
- 3 ½ cups water
- 2 teaspoons oil or ghee
- 1 teaspoon cumin seeds
- 1 onion (finely sliced)
- 1 teaspoon ginger (minced)
- 1 tablespoon garlic (grated)
- 2 teaspoons cilantro
- Salt, chili, and pepper to taste
- ¼ teaspoon turmeric powder
- 1 cup tomatoes (diced)
- ¼ teaspoon garam masala
- 2 tablespoons cilantro

Instructions:

1. Soak chickpeas in 2 cups of water overnight. Drain and set aside.
2. In the Instant Pot, heat oil using the sauté mode. Add cumin seeds, onion, ginger, and garlic. Cook for 5-8 minutes. Add coriander, spices, and chickpeas. Pour 1 ½ cups water and mix well.
3. Close the lid, seal the pressure release, and pressure cook for 30 minutes.
4. Allow natural pressure release.
5. Stir in tomatoes and garam masala, and sauté on high for 5 minutes.
6. Serve with your choice of accompaniment.

❖ Instant Pot Bread Dahi Vada

Cooking Time: 15 minutes

Servings: 4

Ingredients:

- 5 slices of white bread
- 1 cup milk
- 1/4 cup yogurt
- Salt and pepper to taste
- 1 tablespoon semolina
- Raisins, Cashews, Pistachios, and Almonds as needed
- 2 tablespoons oil

Instructions:

1. Remove corners of bread and cut into small squares.
2. Place bread in a large bowl and pour milk over it.
3. Add all other ingredients and mix well. Let it rest.
4. Heat oil in the Instant Pot using the sauté mode.
5. Gently drop vadas into the pot and fry until light brown.
6. Let them cool slightly.
7. Serve with your favorite sauce.

❖ Instant Pot Bread Poha

Cooking Time: 30 minutes

Servings: 1

Ingredients:

- Oil
  - 7 tablespoons hing (asafoetida)
  - 1 teaspoon mustard seeds
  - Curry leaves
  - Salt and pepper
  - Cooked peas (1 cup)
  - Bread
  - Lemon zest

Instructions:

1. Heat oil in the Instant Pot using sauté mode.
2. Add mustard seeds, curry leaves, red chilies, and peas.
3. Cook until golden brown.
4. Serve warm.

❖ Egg Instant Pot Hole

Cook Time: 15 minutes
Servings: 2

Ingredients:

- 2 bread slices
  - 1 egg
  - Butter
  - Coriander

- Salt, pepper, and chili powder

Instructions:

1. Cut a circle from the center of each bread slice.
2. Heat oil in the pot.
3. Place the bread in the pot and crack an egg into the center.
4. Cook for 5 minutes. Serve with salt.

❖ Instant Pot Chili Paneer

Cooking Time: 15 minutes

Ingredients:

- Paneer
- Corn Flour
- All-purpose flour (Maida)
- Salt and pepper
- Oil
- Garlic, chilies, cabbage, and Capsicum

Instructions:

1. In a bowl, mix all ingredients well.
2. Fry paneer until golden brown.
3. In a pan, heat oil and add vegetables and spices. Cook for a while.
4. Serve hot.

❖ Instant Pot Kabab Pea

Cooking Time: 15 minutes

Ingredients:

- Spinach
- Cooked peas
- Garlic and chilies
- Salt and pepper
- 2 slices of bread
- Chickpea flour

Instructions:

1. Blend peas, spinach, ginger, green chilies, and bread to make a paste. Mix in spices. Shape into rounds. Fry in the Instant Pot.
2. Serve hot.

❖ Instant Pot Quesadilla

Cooking Time: 25 minutes

Ingredients:

- Chapatis
- Onion and capsicum (sliced)
- Olives

- Cheese
- Salt and pepper

Instructions:

1. Combine peppers, berries, olives, capsicum, and spices.
2. Fill chapatis with the mixture and fry in the Pot.
3. Serve hot.

❖ Instant Cook Cooked Chili Chicken

Total Time: 35 minutes

Ingredients:

- Oil
- Garlic
- Salt, pepper, and chili powder
- 1 cup shredded chicken
- 1 tomato (minced)
- Basil

Instructions:

1. Add all ingredients to the pot and cook for 10 minutes.
2. Serve garnished as desired.

❖ Instant Pot Coconut Balls

Total Time: 20 minutes

Ingredients:

- 3 cups shredded coconut
  - Condensed milk
  - Ghee
  - Cardamom
  - Sugar

Instructions:

1. Place all ingredients in the Pot and cook for 5 minutes.
2. Let it cool, then shape into small balls. Refrigerate to set.

❖ Instant Pot Cooked Rice Egg

Cooking Time: 30 minutes

Ingredients:

- Oil
  - Egg
  - Boiled rice
  - Ginger and chili
  - Salt and pepper

- Soy sauce

Instructions:

1. Use sauté mode in the pot and add all ingredients.
2. Cook for 15 minutes.
3. Serve hot, garnished with spring onions and coriander leaves.

❖ Instant Pot French Toast Masala Cheese

Preparation Time: 20 minutes

Ingredients:

- Ketchup
- Mayonnaise
- White bread
- Egg whites
- Cheese slices
- Onion
- Salt and pepper

Instructions:

1. Make a herb paste and sauce.
2. Take a slice of bread. Add 2 cheese slices and the sauce paste. Dip in beaten egg whites. Chill for 2-3 minutes.
3. Cook in the pot.

4. Serve hot.

❖ Instant Pot Ghavan

Cook Time: 30 minutes

Ingredients:

- Raw rice
- Salt and pepper
- Oil

Instructions:

1. Soak rice for 1 hour.
2. Blend into a paste and mix in spices.
3. Use the sauté mode in the Pot to spread and cook it in oil.

❖ Instant Pot Bibim Guksuu
Cooking Time: 30 minutes

Ingredients:

- Dried buckwheat noodles

For salad:

- Broccoli (

chopped)
- Cabbage (chopped)
- Cucumber (sliced)
- Carrot
- Boiled peas
- Kimchi

For the sauce:

- Chili paste
- Vinegar
- Soy sauce
- Honey
- Sesame oil

Instructions:

1. Boil the noodles in rolling boiling water and drain the noodles. To cool them off, pass the cold water over the noodles. Drain.
2. In a wide serving dish, place the noodles and combine all the salad ingredients with Korean sauce. Serve after all the ingredients are placed in the bowl.
3. Combine all ingredients well and indulge in chopsticks.

Instant Pot Peanut Gajak:

Cooking Time: 25 minutes

Ingredients:
- Jaggery
- Peanuts

- Ghee

Instructions:

1. Melt jaggery with ghee over low heat in the Instant Pot.
2. Add peanuts and let them cook for a while.
3. Let it cool down.
4. Serve.

Instant Pot Ragi Chakli:

Cooking Time: 25 minutes

Ingredients:

- Ragi Flour
- Besan Flour
- Ginger
- Salt and Pepper
- Oil

Instructions:

1. Knead dried ingredients together, adding oil and necessary water.
2. Form a semi-soft dough. Make chaklis of uniform size.
3. Place chaklis in the preheated Instant Pot.
4. Let them cool, then serve.

Instant Pot Sakkarai Pongal:

Cooking Time: 30 minutes

Ingredients:

- Rice
  - Moong Dal
  - Milk
  - Jaggery
  - Cashew nuts
  - Raisins
  - Cardamom
  - Ghee

Instructions:

1. Soak rice, cook with ghee, and mix with roasted moong dal. Add jaggery and blend thoroughly.
2. Heat ghee, add cashew nuts, raisins, and cardamom. Fry until golden, then mix into the rice mixture.
3. Serve sweet.

Instant Pot Sable Viennois:

Cooking Time: 25 minutes

Ingredients:

- Butter
- Sugar
- Egg whites
- Flour
- Salt
- Vanilla Essence

Instructions:

1. Cream butter and sugar until light and fluffy.
2. Gradually add egg whites and vanilla essence.
3. Sift and gently fold in flour and salt.
4. Pipe and bake in the Instant Pot for 12 minutes.

Instant Pot Indian Chaat:

Cooking Time: 20 minutes

Ingredients:

- Potatoes (2, boiled)
- Chickpeas (1/2 cup, boiled)
- Salt and Pepper
- Black Chaat Masala
- Lime Juice (1 cup)

Instructions:

1. Mix all ingredients together and serve.

Instant Pot Pav Bhaji:

Cooking Time: 30 minutes

Servings: 4

Ingredients:

- 1/2 cup butter
- 1 tablespoon cumin seeds
- 1 red onion (chopped)
- 1/2 capsicum (sliced)
- 1 tablespoon garlic (minced)
- 2 tomatoes (chopped)
- 1 potato (cubed)
- 1 cup chopped cauliflower
- 1/2 cup peas
- 1/2 carrot (chopped)
- Salt, pepper, and red chili to taste
- 1/2 cup water
- 2 tablespoons Pav Bhaji masala
- 1 teaspoon lime zest

Instructions:

1. Chop all vegetables.
2. Turn on the Instant Pot in sauté mode. Add 1 tablespoon of butter, onions, tomatoes, and cumin seeds. Cook for 5-10 minutes.
3. Add all spices. Mix thoroughly.
4. Add all chopped vegetables and water.
5. Cover with a lid and lock the vent. Cancel sauté mode.
6. Cook at manual pressure for 6 minutes.
7. Release pressure naturally.
8. Add masala. Mash and mix with a potato masher.
9. Turn on sauté mode and cook for 2-3 minutes.
10. Add remaining butter and lime zest while simmering.
11. Serve garnished as desired.

Instant Pot Corn with Butter:

Cooking Time: 30 minutes

Servings: 6

Ingredients:

- 6 fresh corn kernels (peeled)
- 1 cup water
- 2 tablespoons butter
- 1 garlic clove (peeled)
- 2 teaspoons powdered paprika
- Salt and chili to taste

- 1 tablespoon powdered onion
- 1 lime

Instructions:

1. Place corn kernels in the Instant Pot.
2. Add 2 cups of water. Set pressure to release for 2-3 minutes after the timer goes off, then use the rapid release technique before opening the lid.
3. Drain the corn in a large bowl.
4. Cover the Instant Pot with a lid and, using a cloth, raise the pot and shake it, flipping it upside down a couple of times, to mix the corn kernels through the butter and spices.

Instant Pot Poha:

Cooking Time: 30 minutes

Servings: 5

Ingredients:

- 1 1/2 cups Poha
- 1 potato (cut into cubes)
- 1 onion (chopped)
- 1/2 cup peas
- Salt, chili, and pepper to taste
- Lime zest

For Tadka:

- 1 tablespoon oil
- 1 teaspoon mustard seeds
- 2 green chilies
- Curry leaves

Instructions:

1. Wash the poha in a bowl for a minute. Drain and set aside.
2. Turn on the Instant Pot to sauté mode. Add the ingredients given under tadka when it becomes hot.
3. Add vegetables and seeds. Cook for 5-10 minutes or until onions become translucent.
4. Add all spices.
5. Cover the lid and cook for 2 minutes on manual mode, then release pressure instantly.
6. Add poha. Mix well and close the lid. Let it sit for 10 minutes.
7. Open the lid and serve with your favorite garnishes.

6

Conclusion

Indian cuisine offers a rich and diverse world of flavors and culinary experiences. While it may seem intimidating with its exotic ingredients and bold spices, it's a journey worth embarking on. Indian food is a fusion of various techniques and mysterious spices, resulting in a tantalizing array of dishes.

Cooking Indian food at home can be a rewarding experience. Understanding the different dishes and flavors that make up Indian cuisine is the first step. The common thread in Indian cooking is the skillful use of spices, which ties together the diverse regional cuisines.

Indian cuisine also provides an excellent option for vegetarians, with a wide variety of dishes featuring ingredients like potatoes, cauliflower, spinach, and eggplant. The judicious application of seasonings and sauces transforms these ingredients into delightful vegetarian meals.

As you start your Indian cooking journey, it's a good idea to keep things simple. This book has provided you with a range of Instant Pot recipes for breakfast, lunch, dinner, snacks, and vegetarian dishes. Instant Pot Indian recipes are not only delicious but also easier to prepare at home. The only challenge you might face is getting to know how to use the Instant Pot effectively. Once you're familiar with it, you'll be on your way to creating authentic Indian dishes in your own kitchen.

www.ingramcontent.com/pod-product-compliance
Lightning Source LLC
LaVergne TN
LVHW020429080526
838202LV00055B/5103